D1518979

TRAILBLAZING WOMEN IN
TRACK AND FIELD

BY KAREN ROSEN

NORWOOD HOUSE PRESS

Cover: Jamaica's Elaine Thompson-Herah wins the women's 200-meter final at the Tokyo Olympics in 2021.

Norwood House Press

For information regarding Norwood House Press, please visit our website at: www.norwoodhousepress.com or call 866-565-2900.

Credits
Editor: Katie Chanez and Patrick Donnelly
Designer: Becky Daum
Fact Checker: Lillian Dondero

PHOTO CREDITS: Cover: © Kyodo/AP Images; © Anastasiia Guseva/iStockphoto, 5; © Ulrik Pedersen/Nur Photo/AP Images, 6; © Library of Congress, 9; © AP Images, 11, 15, 17, 19, 21, 23, 24, 27, 29, 31, 37; © Ron Heflin/AP Images, 34; © Hussein Sayed/AP Images, 39; © Kyodo/AP Images, 41; © David J. Phillip/AP Images, 43; © Kirby Lee/LEEKI/AP Images, 45

Library of Congress Cataloging-in-Publication Data
Names: Rosen, Karen, author.
Title: Trailblazing women in track and field / by Karen Rosen.
Description: Chicago : Norwood House Press, 2023. | Series: Trailblazing female athletes | Includes bibliographical references and index. | Audience: Grades 4-6
Identifiers: LCCN 2022005095 (print) | LCCN 2022005096 (ebook) | ISBN 9781684507511 (hardcover) | ISBN 9781684048045 (paperback) | ISBN 9781684048106 (ebook)
Subjects: LCSH: Women track and field athletes--Biography--Juvenile literature. | Women Olympic athletes--Biography--Juvenile literature.
Classification: LCC GV697.A1 R67 2023 (print) | LCC GV697.A1 (ebook) | DDC 796.42092/52--dc23/eng/20220207
LC record available at https://lccn.loc.gov/2022005095
LC ebook record available at https://lccn.loc.gov/2022005096

Hardcover ISBN: 978-1-68450-751-1
Paperback ISBN: 978-1-68404-804-5

353N—082022
Manufactured in the United States of America in North Mankato, Minnesota.

CONTENTS

GETTING INTO THE GAMES

The ancient Olympic Games began with a footrace. The Games took place almost 2,800 years ago in Olympia, Greece. Athletes took part in competitions including running, jumping, and discus throw. But girls and women were not allowed to compete. Married women could not even watch.

Eventually the ancient Olympics declined in popularity. By 393 CE, the event ended. It was not until 1896 that the modern Olympic Games were founded. Track and field was one of the original sports. However, women were still barred from competing. Baron Pierre de Coubertin had the idea to

The Panathenaic Stadium in Athens, Greece, hosted the first modern Olympics.

restart the Olympics. But he said including women would not be practical, interesting, or proper.

Over time, things began to change. The men who ran sports agreed that some were suitable for women. By the second Olympic Games in 1900, 22 women competed in five sports. However, track and field was not one of them. Some sports officials believed it was too strenuous for women.

By the 1920s some women were tired of waiting. They created an Olympics-like event called the Women's

Athletes compete in the women's 100-meter dash at the Tokyo Olympics in 2021.

World Games. That put pressure on Olympics organizers. Finally, in 1928, women's track and field was added. But women would be limited to five events. Men had 22.

A teenager from the United States won the first women's track gold medal. Betty Robinson was only 16 when she won the 100-meter dash. Hers would be the first of many impressive feats by women in Olympic track and field.

Fanny Blankers-Koen was a Dutch mother of two. In 1948, she earned four gold medals. No woman had won that many golds in a single Olympics before. Twelve years later, Wilma Rudolph emerged as the newest superstar sprinter. The Tennessee native did so despite being unable to walk as a child due to polio. In 1984, the Olympics finally added a women's marathon. It's the longest running event. Joan Benoit's inspiring victory brought more interest to women's long-distance running.

Women continue to push the limits at each new Olympics. In 2021, that included Elaine Thompson-Herah. The record-setting Jamaican sprinter defended her gold medals in the 100- and 200-meter events. She also added another gold in the 4x100-meter relay.

Women's track and field had come a long way over the previous century. However, at the Olympic level it still was not equal. Men had more events than women. Olympic officials finally changed that. They announced men and women would compete in the same number of events at the 2024 Olympics. Many centuries after that first footrace, women would finally be on equal footing.

CHAPTER ONE

BETTY ROBINSON

One day in early 1928 Betty Robinson had to take off running to catch a train. It looked like the high school student would never make it. But she did. One of her teachers happened to be watching. He wanted to confirm if she'd run as fast as it appeared. So, he timed her running down a hallway at their Riverdale, Illinois, school. It turned out she indeed was super-fast. The school didn't have a girls' track team. However, the teacher happened to be an assistant coach on the boys' team. He invited her to join.

Robinson ran in her first meet in March 1928. She soon made the US Olympic team.

Olympic Star

The summer of 1928 was an important one. Women competed in track and field for

Betty Robinson was one of the first American track and field stars.

the first time at the Olympics. The 100-meter dash was the first of five women's events. Four months after her first meet, Robinson won with a time of 12.2 seconds. That was a world record. She also became the first woman to win an Olympic gold medal in the sport. And she was only 16.

Robinson later won a silver medal with the US team in the 4x100-meter relay. Her feats made her a hero back home. Upon her return, the city of Chicago, Illinois, held a parade for her. Nearly 20,000 people came to watch. Olympic women's track was just getting started. Yet nearly 100 years later, after the 2021 Games, Robinson remained the youngest woman to have won gold in the 100-meter race.

Distance Disaster

In 1928, the longest race for women was 800 meters. That is two laps around the track. Lina Radke of Germany won. She even posted a world-record time. The 800 is a challenging race. Runners become tired after racing hard. They often collapse after crossing the finish line. This is also common for men's races. But seeing women collapse alarmed some people. As a result, Olympic officials would not let women run races longer than 200 meters until 1960.

Betty Robinson trains on a rooftop track in New York City.

The Accident

In the summer of 1931, Robinson went flying with her cousin. He had just gotten his pilot's license and had a small airplane. Suddenly, the motor stopped. The plane crashed. Robinson was badly injured. The man who found her thought she was dead. He took her to an undertaker.

To their surprise, Robinson was still alive. She remained in the hospital for 11 weeks. Robinson had no chance to

Babe Didrikson

Babe Didrikson was super athletic. She was extremely versatile, too. Perhaps no athlete in history could match her all-around skills. She was born in Texas in 1911. Didrikson participated in many sports growing up. Eventually she starred in basketball. She also became one of the most successful golfers of her time. Track and field came naturally to her, too. In 1932, Didrikson entered the US Olympic trials. She competed in eight events and won five. However, rules at the time limited women to three individual events in the Olympics. Nonetheless, Didrikson medaled in all three she entered. She won gold in the javelin and 80-meter hurdles. She was second in the high jump.

compete at the 1932 Olympics. One of her legs was 0.5 inches (1.27 cm) shorter than the other. She could not walk normally for two years.

But that did not stop Robinson. She made the 1936 Olympic team. She still could not bend one leg fully. Nonetheless, Robinson won another gold medal, this time in the 4x100-meter relay.

QUICK FACT

Mickey Patterson-Tyler finished third in the 200-meter race in 1948. That made her the first Black woman to win an Olympic medal. But the American almost didn't make the race. She had gotten locked in the dressing room. Her coach got her out just in time.

CHAPTER TWO

FANNY BLANKERS-KOEN

Fanny Blankers-Koen was thought to be too old to run fast. People wrote her mean letters saying she should stay home with her children. They didn't think she should go to the Olympics. Blankers-Koen was eager to prove them wrong.

She was born Francina Koen in the Netherlands in 1918. Few women competed in sports at the time. Women's track and field was not even an Olympic sport yet. But Koen was determined to thrive as a young athlete. By 1935 she had won a national title in the 800-meter run. A year later, Koen made the Dutch Olympic team. She was just 18 years old. Yet Koen posted strong results in two very

Fanny Blankers-Koen often left her competitors in the dust at the end of a race.

different events. She tied for sixth in the Olympic high jump. Her 4x100-meter relay team came in fifth.

It was a promising start. Koen said her Olympic highlight was meeting Jesse Owens. The American star had won four gold medals. Little did she know she would match that gold-medal haul just a few years later.

The Olympics were not held in 1940 and 1944 because of World War II (1939-1945). During that time, Koen married her coach, Jan Blankers. He was a former Olympic triple jumper. They had two children. But Blankers-Koen kept training.

Alice Coachman

Alice Coachman was born in 1923 in Albany, Georgia. As a little girl, she jumped over rags tied together above a dirt road. By 1948 she was the Olympic champion in high jump. This made Coachman the first Black woman to win a gold medal. There was a celebration in Coachman's honor when she got home. However, Georgia was **segregated** at the time. Because she was Black, officials would not let her stand near white athletes. The mayor of Albany would not shake Coachman's hand. Today there is a street in her hometown named Alice Avenue.

Fanny Blankers-Koen was an outstanding high jumper as well as an elite sprinter.

It was not common for mothers to compete in sports at the time. Women often didn't have long careers in sports either. After all, Olympic athletes were not allowed to earn money for competing. Yet Blankers-Koen only seemed to be getting better.

She was 30 years old when she arrived in London, England, for the 1948 Olympics. Newspapers called her "the Flying Housewife." Olympic rules still limited women to only three individual events and a relay. Blankers-Koen was the world record holder in the high jump and the long jump. But she had to skip those events. Instead, she focused on running events.

Blankers-Koen started by winning the 80-meter hurdles and the 100-meter dash. After her **heat** in the 200-meter dash, she grew homesick. Her husband convinced her to keep

QUICK FACT

High jump was one of five women's track and field events at the 1928 Olympics. Canada's Ethel Catherwood won with a height of 5 feet, 2.75 inches (1.59 m). Russia's Mariya Lasitskene won gold in 2021 by clearing 6 feet, 8.25 inches (2.04 m).

Fanny Blankers-Koen clears a hurdle at the 1948 Olympics in London.

competing. She went on to win her third gold medal. Then she finished with the 4x100-meter relay. As the **anchor** leg, Blankers-Koen came from behind to win her fourth gold. Her four gold medals were the most by any athlete in any sport in the 1948 Games.

A few months later Blankers-Koen had another baby. It turned out she had been pregnant during the Olympics. Blankers-Koen proved that women could be mothers and still be champion athletes.

Fanny Blankers-Koen stands atop the podium after winning gold in the women's 100 meters at the 1948 Olympic Games.

CHAPTER THREE

WILMA RUDOLPH

Wilma Rudolph did not have an easy start in life. Born two months early in 1940, she was the 20th of 22 children in her family. They lived in rural Tennessee without a lot of money. Some were surprised she survived her first year. Then, at age four, Rudolph grew very sick. She had a disease called polio.

Rudolph was one of the lucky children to survive polio. However, it left her unable to walk. Doctors thought she'd never recover. But once again Rudolph proved everyone wrong. At the time, Tennessee was segregated. The nearest hospital that would treat Black people was 50 miles (80 km) away. But Rudolph and her mom made the trip each week. Miraculously, Rudolph's leg got better. She was able to walk with braces and special shoes.

Wilma Rudolph was one of the most decorated athletes in US track and field history.

From left, Margaret Matthews, Wilma Rudolph, Mae Faggs, and Isabelle Daniels took the bronze medal in the 4x100-meter relay at the 1956 Olympics.

One day, when Rudolph was 11, her mom found her barefoot and playing basketball. Rudolph no longer needed special braces or shoes to walk. She was on her way to becoming one of the most famous sprinters in history.

As a 16-year-old high school student, Rudolph competed in the 1956 Olympics. Her performance helped the US 4x100-meter team win a bronze medal. The 200-meter sprint wasn't as successful. Rudolph didn't run fast enough to get out of the heats. However, she learned a lot.

Laws in parts of the United States **discriminated** against Black people. But Black women thrived for Team USA in track and field. Many of them trained at Tennessee State University. After the Olympics, the Tennessee State Tigerbelles invited Rudolph to train with them. She eventually became part of the team when she went to college.

Olympic Champion

By the 1960 Olympics, Rudolph was ready to win. Many expected her to win the 100 in Rome, Italy. She was so relaxed that she fell asleep while waiting for her semifinal.

Still, Rudolph won easily and equaled the world record of 11.3 seconds. She was even faster in the final. Her time didn't count as a record because it was **wind-aided**. But her gold medal did. Rudolph also won gold in the 200.

Wyomia Tyus

Wyomia Tyus was not expected to win the 100 meters at the 1964 Olympics in Tokyo, Japan. She had never beaten her teammate Edith McGuire. But Tyus bested McGuire in the Olympic final with a time of 11.2 seconds. Four years later, Tyus won again. The final included four women who shared the world record. Tyus set a new record of 11.0 seconds. That made her the first back-to-back 100-meter champ. Black US athletes Tommie Smith and John Carlos famously protested for racial equality while on the medal stand in 1968. Tyus wore black shorts to show she agreed with them.

Wilma Rudolph cruises to victory in the semifinals of the 200-meter race at the 1960 Rome Olympics.

Last up was the 4x100. Rudolph and the team set a world record in the semifinals. In the final, she was in the anchor position. The last **baton** handoff was clumsy. It took longer than usual. But Rudolph charged ahead to regain the lead. She became the first American woman to win three track and field gold medals at one Olympics. Because of her performance, people began calling Rudolph the "fastest woman in the world." Despite her hard start in life, Rudolph had become one of the sport's great champions.

QUICK FACT

Gail Devers went into the 1992 and 1996 Olympic Games as a favorite to win the 100-meter hurdles. Instead, the US runner won the 100-meter dash twice. She never earned an Olympic medal in the hurdles.

Wilma Rudolph breaks the tape to win the 4x100-meter relay at the 1960 Olympic Games.

CHAPTER FOUR

JOAN BENOIT

Olympic officials had long ago determined that women were not capable of running long distances. Of course, they were wrong. And with each new distance event, new stars emerged to show just how wrong they were.

The women's 800-meter event made its Olympic debut in 1920. But it was not held again until 1960. Twelve years later, a women's 1,500-meter race was added to the Olympic program. But the longest track and field race was not added to the Games until 12 years after that. In 1984, the Olympics finally included a women's marathon. The iconic 26.2-mile race had been a staple on the men's side since the first Olympics in 1896. American Joan Benoit and her Norwegian counterpart, Grete Waitz, were prepared

Joan Benoit was one of the first elite female marathoners.

In 1984, Nawal El Moutawakel of Morocco won the first Olympic gold medal in the women's 400-meter hurdles. In her honor, the King of Morocco ordered that all girls born that day be named Nawal.

to make the Olympic women's marathon a must-see race, too.

Benoit was born in 1957 in Cape Elizabeth, Maine. After she broke her leg in a skiing accident, running helped her heal.

Breaking into Boston

Bobbi Gibb tried to enter the 1966 Boston Marathon. Organizers said no women were allowed. But that didn't stop her. She hid in a bush near the starting line, then snuck out and ran the race. A year later, Kathrine Switzer registered for the race. She signed her name K. V. Switzer. Thinking that was a man's name, race officials accepted her. On race day, she felt welcomed by the male runners as they warmed up. However, after about 4 miles (6.4 km), an official jumped onto the course. He tried to force Switzer out of the marathon. But he was not able to rip off her race number. Switzer got away and finished the race. She campaigned for women to be allowed to run distance races. Finally, in 1972, the Boston Marathon officially accepted female runners.

In 1979, she won her first Boston Marathon. Her time of 2:35:15 was the fastest ever for an American woman. And in the coming years, Benoit ran faster and faster.

With the first Olympic women's marathon coming up, Benoit was looking like a contender to win a gold medal. There was one problem. For as fast as Benoit ran, she'd still have to beat Waitz.

Waitz had set the world record in her first-ever marathon. In 1983, one year before the first Olympic women's marathon, Waitz won the first official marathon world title. Going into the 1984 Olympics, Waitz had never lost a marathon. However, Benoit and Waitz had never met head-to-head. And by the time they did at the 1984 Olympics, Benoit had taken over as the world record holder.

QUICK FACT

Men have been pole vaulting at the Olympics since 1896. Women finally made their Olympic debut in 2000. Stacy Dragila of the United States **cleared** 15 feet, 1 inch (4.6 m) to win the gold.

Joan Benoit ran far ahead of the pack during the 1984 Olympic marathon in Los Angeles.

Everything was setting up for an epic showdown at the 1984 Games in Los Angeles, California.

Olympic Rivalry

On the morning before the race, Waitz woke up with a sore back. She could not stand up straight. She felt better in time for the marathon. But this was Benoit's day. She took the lead in the third mile. Soon Benoit left Waitz—and the other runners—behind.

It was a risky strategy for Benoit, especially against such an accomplished runner as Waitz and on a humid day when the high temperature reached 90 degrees Fahrenheit (32°C). Benoit was all alone when she emerged from the tunnel into the Olympic stadium. The crowd of more than 77,000 was waiting. Waving her white cap, Benoit crossed the finish

Jackie Joyner-Kersee

Jackie Joyner-Kersee was born in 1962. She was named after First Lady Jacqueline Kennedy. Her grandmother predicted she would be "first lady" of something. Joyner-Kersee made her mark in the **heptathlon**. It has seven track and field events. The competition is said to determine the world's best female athlete. Unfortunately, Joyner-Kersee narrowly missed the gold at the 1984 Los Angeles Olympics, but she left no question as to who was the best in 1988 and 1992. Three decades later her world record of 7,291 points still stood. Heptathletes must be good across each event. Joyner-Kersee was better than that in the long jump. She took the gold in the event in 1988 and won bronze in 1992 and 1996.

line in 2:24:52, the third-fastest time ever for a woman. She entered the history books as the first woman to win an Olympic marathon. Waitz, who was about 400 meters behind, won the silver medal.

Benoit's dominant performance helped make women's long distance running popular. And she kept on going. Later running under her married name of Joan Benoit Samuelson, she raced in seven Olympic marathon trials. In 2010, at age 53, she missed qualifying for her eighth by just 110 seconds.

Joan Benoit takes a victory lap after winning the women's marathon at the 1984 Olympics.

CHAPTER FIVE

ELAINE THOMPSON-HERAH

Fewer than 3 million people live in Jamaica. Yet the small Caribbean island nation has developed a great sprinting tradition. Among many excellent sprinters, Elaine Thompson-Herah stands out.

Thompson-Herah was born in Banana Ground, Jamaica, in 1992. She started running at age six. When sent to the store, she would sprint there and back. She did not want to miss her favorite cartoons. But Thompson-Herah's family was not that interested in sports. In high school, she was good, but not great at track. She was once left off her team because of bad behavior. She joined the track team again

Elaine Thompson-Herah followed a long line of outstanding sprinters to come from Jamaica.

American hurdler Dalilah Muhammad won gold in the 400 meters at the 2016 Olympics. She set a world record in the event in 2019. Then teammate Sydney McLaughlin broke that record in 2021. At that summer's Olympics, they both ran under the record again. However, McLaughlin was a little faster. Now each had an Olympic gold medal.

in college. That's when she began to emerge as a superstar.

Becoming the Best

Thompson-Herah broke onto the global scene at the 2015 World Championships. She finished second in the 200. Her teammate Shelly-Ann

Florence Griffith Joyner

Elaine Thompson-Herah ended 2021 as the second-fastest woman of all time in the 100- and 200-meter races. That meant Florence Griffith Joyner's long reign at the top continued. She won three gold medals and a silver at the 1988 Olympics. That year "Flo-Jo" also set world records of 10.49 seconds in the 100 and 21.34 seconds in the 200. In addition to her speed, Griffith Joyner was also known for her stylish outfits and long, colorful fingernails.

Fraser-Pryce was faster. Known as the "Pocket Rocket," Fraser-Pryce was a two-time Olympic champion at 100 meters. To be the best in the world, Thompson-Herah would need to beat her all-time great teammate.

Elaine Thompson-Herah reacts to winning the 100-meter finals at the 2016 Rio Olympics.

At the 2016 Rio Olympics, she did just that. Fraser-Pryce was favored to win another 100-meter gold. Instead, Thompson-Herah charged to victory. Fraser-Pryce took third. Thompson-Herah also won the 200. She earned a silver in the 4x100 relay.

Thompson-Herah appeared to be the next great Jamaican sprinter. However, after the Games she struggled with an

Sifan Hassan was born in Ethiopia. She moved to the Netherlands as a **refugee** in 2008. At the Tokyo Olympics in 2021, she was the first athlete to win medals in the 1,500, the 5,000, and the 10,000 meters in the same Olympics.

Achilles injury. She did not win a medal in any individual event at the 2017 or 2019 World Championships. Then her injury came back in 2020. Thompson-Herah could not sprint or even walk at times. However, that year's Olympics were pushed back to 2021

Valerie Adams

Everything about Valerie Adams is big. Her family is big, with 18 kids. And she is big too, standing 6-foot-4. As a kid, Adams was teased due to her height. But she grew into a powerful woman and historically good shot putter. Adams competed in five Olympics for New Zealand. She won medals in four of them, including two golds. In 2017, Adams was the youngest New Zealander to be appointed a Dame by her country. In New Zealand, to become a Dame is one of the greatest honors awarded to any woman.

Elaine Thompson-Herah recovered from her injuries in time to participate in the Tokyo Olympics in 2021.

due to the COVID-19 **pandemic**. That gave Thompson-Herah more time to recover.

And did she ever. In Tokyo, Japan, she became the first woman to win back-to-back Olympic crowns in the 100 and 200. In the 100 meters, Thompson-Herah set an Olympic record of 10.61 seconds—despite running into the wind. In the 200, she clocked 21.53 seconds. That moved her into second place on the all-time list. When Jamaica won the 4x100-meter relay, Thompson-Herah had her third gold of the Games. It was her fifth overall.

QUICK FACT

Yulimar Rojas broke the world record in the triple jump at the Tokyo Olympics in 2021. Rojas won Venezuela's only gold medal at the Games. She was also the first Venezuelan woman to become an Olympic champion in any sport. Her gold medal was Venezuela's first in track and field.

And she wasn't done yet. After the Olympics, Thompson-Herah raced at a meet in Oregon. Her time of 10.54 seconds was the second-best ever. The performance surprised even her. When told her time, Thompson-Herah said she'd felt kind of slow!

Women keep raising the bar as they challenge themselves and their competitors to advance the sport of track and field.

Women had to fight to be accepted into track and field. Even now they continue to seek equality. Yet throughout the sport's history, women have continued to push the limits. They have shown the world they are capable of championship performances. Before long, more athletes will come along to run even faster and perform even better.

GLOSSARY

anchor
the last of four runners on a relay team

baton
a short stick that runners carry in a relay race and pass to each other

cleared
to have successfully made it over the bar in the high jump or pole vault

discriminated
to have treated a person or group of people unfairly based on characteristics such as gender or race

heat
an early round in a running event

heptathlon
a track and field event that includes the 100-meter hurdles, high jump, shot put, 200 meters, long jump, javelin throw, and 800 meters

pandemic
an outbreak of a disease that occurs over a wide geographic area and typically affects a significant proportion of the population

refugee
a person forced to leave his or her home to escape danger

segregated
to have separated a group of people from everyone else

wind-aided
a result that counts in competition but is not eligible for records because the conditions are too windy

FOR MORE INFORMATION

Books

Kimmel, Allison Crotzer. *Unbeatable Betty: Betty Robinson, The First Female Olympic Track & Field Gold Medalist.* New York, NY: HarperCollins, 2020.

Pimentel, Annette Bay. *Girl Running: Bobbi Gibb and the Boston Marathon.* New York, NY: Nancy Paulsen Books, 2018.

Williams-Garcia, Rita. *She Persisted: Florence Griffith Joyner.* New York, NY: Philomel Books, 2021.

Websites

International Olympic Committee (IOC)
(olympic.org)
The IOC is the governing body of the Olympic Games.

USA Track and Field
(usatf.org)
This is the online home for the United States track and field team.

World Athletics
(worldathletics.org)
This site provides news and results from the world of track and field.

INDEX

ABOUT THE AUTHOR

Karen Rosen was a trailblazer as a "paper girl" in Auburn, Alabama. Her father was an Olympic track and field coach. Rosen went to her first Olympic Games in Montreal, Canada, in 1976 on a family vacation and worked for ABC at the 1984 Los Angeles Games. As a journalist, she has written about every summer and winter Olympics since 1992.